INDIANAPOLIS COLTS

BY ROBERT COOPER

An Imprint of Abdo Publishing
abdobooks.com

abdobooks.com

Printed in the United States of America, North Mankato, Minnesota
042019
092019

Cover Photo: Wesley Hitt/Getty Images Sport/Getty Images
Interior Photos: David Duprey/AP Images, 5; Kevork Djansezian/AP Images, 7; Chris Carlson/AP Images, 9; William A. Smith/AP Images, 11; NFL Photos/AP Images, 12, 14, 19, 23; Harold Matosian/AP Images, 17; Peter Read Miller/AP Images, 21; Al Messerschmidt/AP Images, 24, 43; George Widman/AP Images, 27; Adam Nadel/AP Images, 29; Lenny Ignelzi/AP Images, 31; Greg Trott/AP Images, 35; Michael Conroy/AP Images, 37, 39; AJ Mast/AP Images, 40

Editor: Patrick Donnelly
Series Designer: Craig Hinton

Library of Congress Control Number: 2018965344

Publisher's Cataloging-in-Publication Data

Names: Cooper, Robert, author.
Title: Indianapolis Colts / by Robert Cooper
Description: Minneapolis, Minnesota: Abdo Publishing, 2020 | Series: Inside the NFL | Includes online resources and index.
Identifiers: ISBN 9781532118494 (lib. bdg.) | ISBN 9781532172670 (ebook)
Subjects: LCSH: Indianapolis Colts (Football team)--Juvenile literature. | National Football League--Juvenile literature. | Football teams--Juvenile literature. | American football--Juvenile literature.
Classification: DDC 796.33264--dc23

TABLE OF CONTENTS

CHAPTER 1
WINNING BIG 4

CHAPTER 2
WINNING EARLY AND OFTEN 10

CHAPTER 3
MAINTAINING EXCELLENCE 16

CHAPTER 4
MOVING DAY 22

CHAPTER 5
CREATING A DYNASTY 28

CHAPTER 6
A LUCKY BREAK 34

TIMELINE 42
QUICK STATS 44
QUOTES AND ANECDOTES 45
GLOSSARY 46
MORE INFORMATION 47
ONLINE RESOURCES 47
INDEX 48
ABOUT THE AUTHOR 48

CHAPTER 1

WINNING BIG

For Peyton Manning and the Indianapolis Colts, the 2006 season opener was special. The Colts' opponent that day was the New York Giants. Their quarterback was Eli Manning. It was the first National Football League (NFL) game in which the starting quarterbacks were brothers.

Older brother Peyton got the best of this contest. The Colts defeated the Giants 26–21 at Giants Stadium in East Rutherford, New Jersey. That historic start was just one of many highlights for Colts' fans during the 2006 season. After beating the Giants, Indianapolis went on to finish 12–4 during the regular season. The Colts then won three playoff games to qualify for Super Bowl XLI.

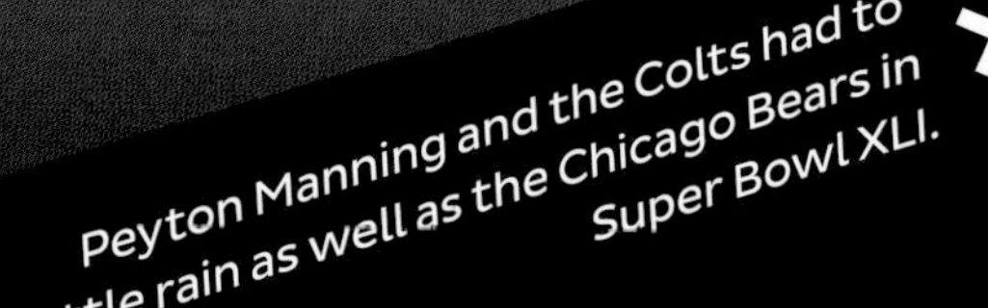

Peyton Manning and the Colts had to battle rain as well as the Chicago Bears in Super Bowl XLI.

18

The Super Bowl was a chance for Peyton Manning to prove his critics wrong. Throughout his career, he had been one of the league's top quarterbacks. He had already set a handful of NFL single-season passing records in his career, including 49 touchdown passes in 2004. However, his teams had continually come up short in the playoffs.

This time around, Manning and the Colts would have to battle more than just the Chicago Bears to get the job done. Super Bowl XLI was played in Miami. The game was scheduled there because Miami usually has nice weather in February. But on this day, heavy rain fell as the teams took the field to start the game. And the Colts, who play their home games indoors, were used to ideal conditions.

The game got off to a terrible start for the Colts. Chicago's Devin Hester returned the opening kickoff 92 yards for a touchdown. Then Manning was intercepted on the Colts' first possession.

The Colts finally broke through on their next possession when

MR. CLUTCH

Kicker Adam Vinatieri is no stranger to pressure moments in the Super Bowl. Prior to joining the Indianapolis Colts in 2006, he won three Super Bowls with the New England Patriots. Vinatieri kicked game-winning field goals to clinch two of those NFL titles.

Colts kicker Adam Vinatieri, *bottom*, could not stop Bears kick returner Devin Hester on the opening play of Super Bowl XLI.

Manning found star wide receiver Reggie Wayne for a 53-yard touchdown. However, the rain caused the Colts' holder to drop the snap on the extra-point attempt, which was unsuccessful.

The sloppiness continued. Each team had three turnovers in the first half. Even the Colts' reliable kicker, Adam Vinatieri, missed a field-goal attempt in the second quarter. The rain did not let up in the second half. But neither did the Colts. They slowly took control of the game. Going into the fourth quarter, they held a 22–17 lead.

The Bears began a drive early in the fourth quarter. A touchdown would have given them the lead. Even a field goal would have made the game uncomfortably close for Indianapolis. Instead, an unlikely Colts player stepped up.

Cornerback Kelvin Hayden was the Colts' second-round draft pick in 2005. In two seasons he had not intercepted a pass. But on the fourth play of the Bears' drive, Hayden stepped in front of a pass from Chicago quarterback Rex Grossman. He returned the interception 56 yards for a touchdown. Indianapolis held on to win Super Bowl XLI 29–17.

There had been many key individual efforts in the game. Rookie running back Joseph Addai rushed for 77 yards on 19 carries. He also caught 10 passes for 66 yards. His backfield mate, Dominic Rhodes, rushed 21 times for 113 yards and one touchdown. Vinatieri kicked three field goals. His 49 points that postseason set an NFL record.

In the end, however, Manning was the game's star player. Despite the rainy weather, the Colts quarterback completed 25 of 38 passes for 247 yards and a touchdown. For his effort, Manning was named the game's Most Valuable Player (MVP). He had finally won—and starred in—the NFL's biggest game.

Indianapolis cornerback Kelvin Hayden intercepts a crucial pass in the fourth quarter of Super Bowl XLI.

Another important figure on the Colts' sideline cemented his place in history that day. Tony Dungy became the first black head coach to win a Super Bowl.

Winning a Super Bowl was not new for the Colts. They had beaten the Dallas Cowboys to win Super Bowl V in 1971. However, that was back before most fans had given any thought to the idea of an NFL team calling Indianapolis home.

CHAPTER 2

WINNING EARLY AND OFTEN

The first Baltimore Colts team began play in the All-America Football Conference (AAFC) in 1947. In 1950 the Colts and two other AAFC teams joined the larger NFL. The Cleveland Browns and San Francisco 49ers thrived after the move to the NFL. Both teams still exist today. The Colts, however, disbanded because of financial problems after just one season in the NFL.

Behind strong local support, Baltimore soon got a second chance to host professional football. In 1953 the NFL awarded the city a new team to replace the Dallas Texans, who had folded the season before. The new team was also named the Colts. The name paid tribute to the city's rich history in horse racing.

Weeb Ewbank, standing, meets with his quarterbacks, including Johnny Unitas, right, in 1959.

Legendary Colts quarterback Johnny Unitas, shown in 1970, spent 17 years with the Colts.

The new Colts had a losing record in each of their first four seasons. But when they hired Weeb Ewbank as head coach in 1954, a brighter future at least looked possible.

Ewbank began adding talented players to the Colts' roster, and the team slowly improved. After going 3–9 in 1954, the Colts finished 5–6–1 in 1955 and 5–7 in 1956. More important than the 1956 record, however, was the emergence of rookie quarterback Johnny Unitas. The 1956 season would be the last losing season the Colts would experience for several years.

Unitas had guided the team to a 3–4 record in seven starts as a rookie. He greatly improved during his second season. The Colts finished 1957 with a record of 7–5. That began a streak of 15 consecutive non-losing seasons in Baltimore.

Unitas led the Colts all the way to the NFL Championship Game in 1958. The Colts played against the New York Giants at Yankee Stadium in New York City. A national audience watched on television. At the time, it was the most-watched game ever. The fans picked a good one to follow. The back-and-forth drama lasted all the way down to the end of regulation.

In the final two minutes, Unitas led the Colts 73 yards down the field. Colts kicker Steve Myhra hit the game-tying field goal with seven seconds left. The teams went to sudden-death overtime. That meant that the first team to score would win.

The Colts stopped the Giants on the first possession of overtime. Then Unitas took over once again. He led the Colts 80 yards down the field on 13 plays. The Colts secured the win when fullback Alan Ameche scored on a 1-yard touchdown dive.

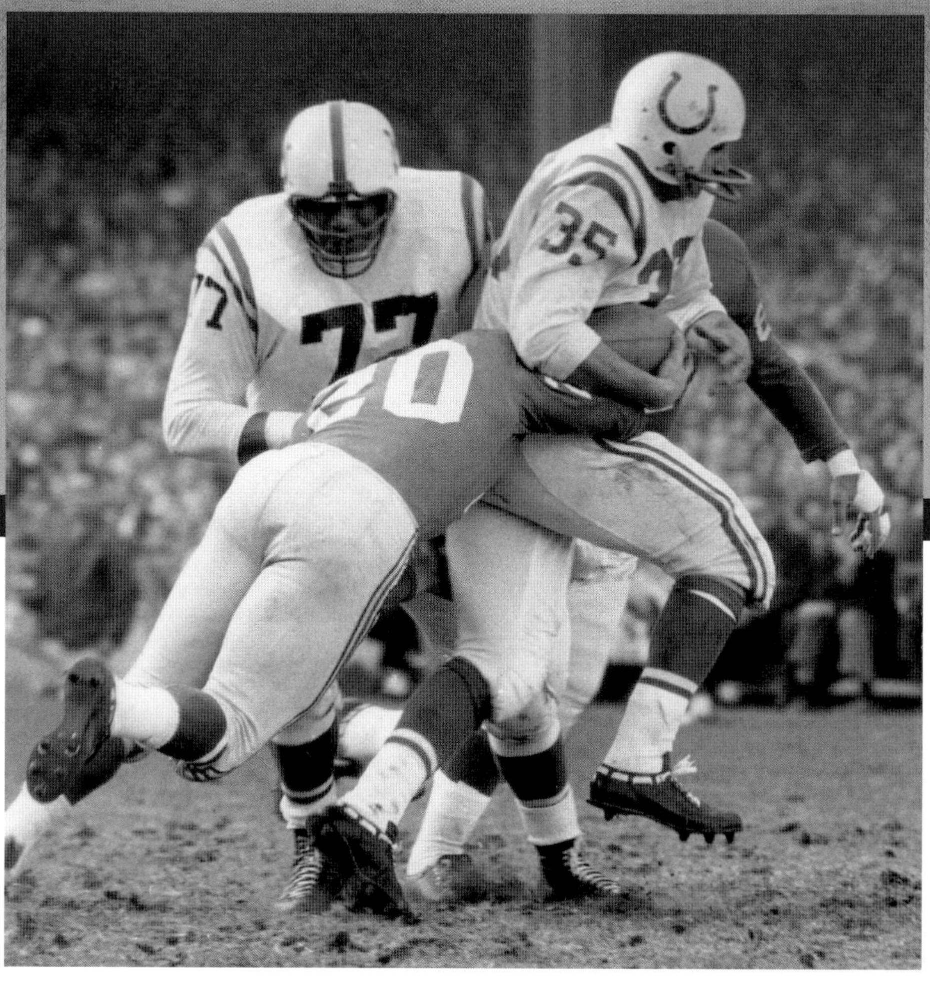

Colts fullback Alan Ameche (35) is slowed by New York Giants defensive back Jimmy Patton in the 1958 NFL Championship Game.

Many consider the contest to be the greatest NFL game ever played. Professional football took off in popularity in the years following the game.

The Colts returned to the NFL Championship Game in 1959. They once again faced the Giants, but this time in Baltimore.

Unitas led the Colts with two passing touchdowns and one rushing touchdown. With their 31–16 win, the Colts successfully defended their NFL title.

Ewbank had helped build the Colts team. However, he would not finish his career there. The Colts fired Ewbank after the 1962 season and he jumped leagues to coach the New York Jets of the rival American Football League (AFL).

A HISTORIC RUN

Quarterback Johnny Unitas set an NFL record by throwing a touchdown pass in 47 consecutive games. His streak was finally stopped in Baltimore's 10–3 win at Los Angeles on December 11, 1960. The record lasted more than 50 years until New Orleans Saints quarterback Drew Brees surpassed Unitas on October 7, 2012. Brees's streak was snapped later that season at 54 games.

Ewbank became the only head coach to win championships with teams from both the NFL and the AFL. He would later come back to be a thorn in the side of the Colts, too. However, in 1963, Baltimore was more concerned with finding a new head coach. The team decided to go with 33-year-old Don Shula. He became the youngest head coach in NFL history at the time. Decades later, he would retire as one of the best NFL head coaches of all time.

CHAPTER 3

MAINTAINING EXCELLENCE

Under new head coach Don Shula, Baltimore returned to the NFL Championship Game in 1964. However, this game was much less enjoyable for the Colts than the previous ones. Baltimore was shut out by the Cleveland Browns 27–0.

Beginning with the 1966 season, the NFL champion began playing the AFL champion in what later became known as the Super Bowl. The Colts played in their first Super Bowl following the 1968 season.

Johnny Unitas only played in five games during that season because of an elbow injury. However, backup Earl Morrall took over and played so well that he was named the NFL MVP. Heading into Super Bowl III, the Colts were heavy favorites against the AFL's New York Jets.

Colts players carry coach Don Shula off the field after the team won the 1964 NFL Western Division title.

Jets star quarterback Joe Namath had other ideas, though. Before the game, he publicly guaranteed that the Jets would win. Weeb Ewbank, who was coaching the Jets, wasn't happy with Namath's boast. Few observers believed an AFL team could compete with the NFL champion at the time. The Colts were also coming off a dominant 13–1 regular season.

Namath lived up to his word, though. He led the Jets to a 13–0 third-quarter lead. In desperation, an injured Unitas came out and tried to save the game for the Colts. He threw a touchdown pass, but it was not enough. The Jets won 16–7.

Shula guided the Colts to a 73–26–4 record during his seven years with the team, including playoffs. However, he was unable to win a Super Bowl. He left after the 1969 season to coach the Miami Dolphins and was replaced by offensive coordinator Don McCafferty.

The new decade brought more than just a coaching change to Baltimore. The NFL completed its merger with the AFL that year. The 10 AFL teams formed the American Football Conference (AFC). However, to balance the conferences, three NFL teams had to join them in the AFC. Those three were the Cleveland Browns, the Pittsburgh Steelers, and the Colts.

Offensive tackle Bob Vogel walks off the field during the Colts' 16–7 loss to the New York Jets in Super Bowl III.

With their new head coach and now playing in the AFC, the Colts went 11–2–1 and reached their second Super Bowl. They played the Dallas Cowboys. Unitas threw a 75-yard touchdown pass in the game. The ball actually bounced off one Colts receiver and then a Cowboys defender before John Mackey pulled it in and ran for the touchdown. However, Unitas later had to leave the game due to injury.

BRINGING A CROWD

The Colts had many future Hall of Fame players during their run of success in the 1950s and 1960s. They included wide receiver Raymond Berry, running back/receiver Lenny Moore, tight end John Mackey, defensive linemen Art Donovan and Gino Marchetti, and offensive lineman Jim Parker. However, Johnny Unitas was the ultimate star of the Baltimore Colts. He was inducted into the Pro Football Hall of Fame in 1979.

Unitas also headlined a group of Colts players who were named to the NFL's fiftieth anniversary team in 1969. A group of 36 Hall of Fame voters selected the team. The first team also included Mackey and Marchetti. Berry and Donovan made the second team, while Moore made the third team.

Dallas and Baltimore combined for a Super Bowl–record 11 turnovers that day. It was a sloppy game with an exciting finish. With 7:35 left, Baltimore's Tom Nowatzke rushed for a 2-yard touchdown to tie the game at 13–13. Dallas had the ball at midfield in the final two minutes, looking to set up a game-winning field goal. However, Colts linebacker Mike Curtis intercepted Cowboys quarterback Craig Morton and returned the ball to the Dallas 28-yard line with 59 seconds left. Three plays later, Baltimore's Jim O'Brien kicked a game-winning 32-yard field goal. The Colts had won Super Bowl V 16–13.

The winning ways in Baltimore would not last, however. Unitas was traded to the San Diego Chargers in 1973. When he retired after the 1974 season, he held 22 NFL records.

Quarterback Bert Jones led the Colts to three division titles in the mid-1970s.

His unprecedented passing skills had changed the NFL forever. In his career, Unitas completed 2,830 passes for 40,239 yards and 290 touchdowns.

The Colts won the AFC East in 1975, 1976, and 1977 with Ted Marchibroda as the head coach and Bert Jones at quarterback. However, they went 0–3 in the playoffs. In fact, the Colts would not win another playoff game until 1995. By then, they would no longer be the Baltimore Colts.

CHAPTER 4

MOVING DAY

On March 28, 1984, Colts owner Robert Irsay approved a secret mission. In the middle of the night, 15 green and yellow Mayflower moving trucks showed up at the Colts' Baltimore training complex. The movers packed up all of the team's things and drove away. The Colts were moving to Indianapolis, Indiana.

The move came as a shock to Colts fans. Irsay had been at odds with the local government and news media for some time. But as people speculated about whether he would try to move the team, Irsay had promised to never do that. The fans felt betrayed when the team left. They were even more irked about how it happened: in secret, in the middle of the night.

Colts running back Eric Dickerson carries the ball during the 1987 playoffs.

COLTS
29

The Colts moved into the spacious Hoosier Dome when they relocated to Indianapolis.

Many former Baltimore Colts fans are still sour over the move to this day. However, the city did get a new team in 1996 when the Cleveland Browns moved to Maryland to become the Baltimore Ravens.

An open house at the Colts' new facility in Indianapolis drew 10,000 visitors. When season tickets were offered, the team received 143,000 inquiries in two weeks. Victories were rare for the Colts during their early seasons in Indianapolis. They won a total of only 12 games during their first three seasons after the move. The Indianapolis Colts had their first winning record in 1987. That was partially due to the addition of star running back Eric Dickerson.

The Colts started the season 0–2. Their third game was cancelled due to a player strike. The team then won two of their next three games with replacement players. The regular players rejoined the team for an October 25 game against the Patriots. The Colts traded for Dickerson on October 31. Dickerson rushed for at least 100 yards in six of the last eight games that season as the Colts finished 9–6, winning the AFC East title before losing to the Browns 38–21 in the playoffs.

The Colts didn't reach the postseason again until 1995. Ted Marchibroda returned as the team's head coach in 1992. He had coached the Colts in Baltimore from 1975 to 1979 and won three division titles in that span. Alongside a quarterback with a memorable nickname, Marchibroda guided the Colts to a 9–7 record in his first year back at the helm.

Quarterback Jim Harbaugh was called "Captain Comeback" because he rallied the Colts to several come-from-behind victories. In Week 2 the Colts fell behind the New York Jets 24–3 in the third quarter. Harbaugh came off the bench and rallied the Colts to a 27–24 overtime win. Later that season, Harbaugh helped the Colts make up a 21-point deficit against the Miami Dolphins. The Colts scored 21 straight points in the second half and ended up beating the Dolphins 27–24 in overtime.

A PAIR OF HALL OF FAMERS

During their time in Indianapolis, the Colts have had a pair of Hall of Fame running backs. The first was Eric Dickerson. He arrived in Indianapolis in 1987. He was immediately successful. Dickerson rushed for 1,659 yards during the 1988 season. He played three more seasons with the Colts before finishing his career with the Los Angeles Raiders and the Atlanta Falcons. Dickerson rushed for 13,259 yards in his career and was inducted into the Pro Football Hall of Fame in 1999.

The second Hall of Famer was running back Marshall Faulk. He proved to be a force for the Colts during his five-year tenure with the team. He was named to three Pro Bowls during his time in Indianapolis, which lasted from 1994 to 1998. Faulk rushed for 1,000 yards in four of his five seasons with the Colts. Faulk finished his career with the St. Louis Rams. He played seven seasons and won a Super Bowl with the Rams. Faulk went into the Pro Football Hall of Fame in 2011.

Following the 1995 regular season, the Colts won two playoff games, both on the road. First they beat the San Diego Chargers 35–20 in the wild-card round. They then upset the top-seeded Kansas City Chiefs 10–7 in the divisional playoffs. Their string of good fortune ran out against the Pittsburgh Steelers, however. The Colts lost 20–16 at Pittsburgh in the AFC Championship Game.

The Colts were unable to build their success from the 1995 season into another Super Bowl appearance. They went 9–7 in 1996 but lost again to the Steelers, this time in the first round of the playoffs. In 1997, the Colts struggled to a 3–13 record.

"Captain Comeback" Jim Harbaugh led the Colts back to the AFC Championship Game after the 1995 season.

Although the Colts were not always fun to watch during that 1997 season, all of that losing did pay off. Because they had the worst record in the league, the team got the top pick in the 1998 NFL Draft. With that selection, the Colts would change the future of their franchise.

CHAPTER 5

CREATING A DYNASTY

With the first pick in the 1998 NFL Draft, the Indianapolis Colts selected Peyton Manning. He had been a star quarterback at the University of Tennessee. His father, Archie, had been a star quarterback for the New Orleans Saints during the 1970s. With Peyton the Colts now had a superstar player to build their team around for many years to come.

With Manning at quarterback and new head coach Jim Mora on the sidelines, the Colts had high hopes for the 1998 season. Manning played well as a rookie. He threw for 3,739 yards and 26 touchdowns and was named to the all-rookie team. However, he also threw 28 interceptions as the Colts finished a lowly 3–13.

Peyton Manning stands with NFL Commissioner Paul Tagliabue at the 1998 NFL Draft.

MANNING
18

But improvement for Manning and the Colts came quickly. After splitting their first four games in 1999, they went on an 11-game winning streak. They finished 13–3 and won the AFC East title. Manning again threw 26 touchdown passes but cut his interceptions to 15 and made his first Pro Bowl appearance.

Though the Colts lost to the Tennessee Titans at home in the divisional round of the playoffs that year, they used 1999 as a springboard to an incredible run. The Colts won 115 games from 2000 to 2009, making them the winningest team in the NFL during that decade.

Much of the Colts' success during that time was due to their high-powered offense. They had selected wide receiver Marvin Harrison in the first round of the 1996 draft. Manning and Harrison connected for 112 regular-season touchdowns in their 11 years playing together. That is the most ever by a wide receiver-quarterback tandem. Manning also had star receiver Reggie Wayne and star tight end Dallas Clark to pass to during much of that time.

Manning quickly became known for having one of the strongest and most accurate throwing arms in the NFL. But he did not always need to pass. The Colts selected running back Edgerrin James with their first-round draft pick in 1999.

Manning hands the ball off to Edgerrin James during a 2004 game. Manning and James played together for seven years.

In seven seasons with the Colts, he was selected to four Pro Bowls. His replacement, Joseph Addai, made the Pro Bowl in 2007.

Despite having a dominant offense, the Colts were unable to reach a Super Bowl during Manning's early years. Mora had helped make the Colts winners. But to take the next step, the team believed it needed new direction.

EPIC RIVALS

Throughout the early and mid-2000s, the Indianapolis Colts and the New England Patriots played in many epic games. Part of the reason these games drew so much interest was because of the quarterbacks. Many NFL experts consider Peyton Manning of the Colts and New England's Tom Brady the two best of their generation.

Manning often put up better stats than Brady. However, in the big games, Brady always seemed to win. The Patriots beat the Colts in the 2003 AFC Championship Game and the 2004 playoffs.

The tide finally turned in the 2006 playoffs. With about two minutes left in the AFC Championship Game, the Colts trailed the Patriots by three points. Manning then led the Colts 80 yards down the field for a touchdown. The Colts held on to win 38–34. Two weeks later, they beat the Bears in Super Bowl XLI.

The Colts fired Mora after the 2001 season. The Tampa Bay Buccaneers had fired their head coach, Tony Dungy, around the same time. As it turned out, Dungy was the perfect fit to take over in Indianapolis.

One of Dungy's first tasks was to fix the Colts' defense. Indianapolis had allowed more than 30 points per game during the 2001 season. Even their second-ranked offense could not make up for that. The Colts had gone 6–10 during Mora's last season.

The Colts' defense steadily improved during the 2000s. Much of that was due to the addition of star players such as defensive end Dwight Freeney and safety Bob Sanders. Together with Manning's high-octane offense, they eventually turned the Colts into champions. In Dungy's fifth season with the Colts, they won Super Bowl XLI by defeating the Chicago Bears 29–17.

The Dungy era came to a close in Indianapolis after the 2008 season. His longtime assistant Jim Caldwell replaced him. Caldwell got off to a fast start. The Colts won their first 14 games of the 2009 season. They had a shot to become the third team to complete a regular season undefeated, but Caldwell rested his starters in the final two games and the Colts lost both. Still, Manning won his fourth NFL MVP Award after the season.

In the playoffs, the Colts rolled through the Baltimore Ravens and the New York Jets. They finally met their match in Super Bowl XLIV. The New Orleans Saints capped off their best season ever with a 31–17 victory over the Colts. Following that Super Bowl loss, change was on the horizon for Indianapolis.

CHAPTER 6

A LUCKY BREAK

Following the 14–2 season in 2009, Colts fans had the pleasure of watching Peyton Manning play quarterback for one more year. In 2010 the Colts went 10–6. Though that was good enough to qualify for the playoffs, it marked the first season since 2002 in which Indianapolis had not won at least 12 games. The Colts bowed out of the playoffs quickly, losing to the New York Jets in the wild-card round.

Manning was sidelined with a neck injury in 2011. The Colts held out hope that he would return to the lineup at some point that season, but it never happened. And Indianapolis suffered. The Colts lost their first 13 games of the season and finished with the worst record in the league at 2–14.

Andrew Luck throws his first career touchdown pass, a 4-yard toss to Donnie Avery at Chicago in 2012.

Riddell
12
NFL
Wilson

That season signaled a new reality for the Colts. Without Manning, the Indianapolis offense scored 243 points, which was fourth worst in the NFL that season. Manning was 35 years old and wouldn't be around forever. So the Colts decided to start over. In March 2012 they released Manning. The amazing run was over.

The Colts also made other big changes. They hired Ryan Grigson as their new general manager and Chuck Pagano as head coach. Indianapolis went into the 2012 NFL Draft looking for a replacement for Manning. The Colts had their choice of any of the top college quarterbacks. They used the No. 1 pick in the draft to select Andrew Luck from Stanford University. The son of a former NFL quarterback, Luck received praise for his strong arm, football knowledge, and decision-making skills.

With a handful of key players remaining from the Manning era, the Colts found success quickly with Luck in 2012. The new quarterback quickly developed a relationship with reliable receiver Reggie Wayne, one of Manning's favorite targets.

But after three games in 2012, Pagano was diagnosed with leukemia. The disease forced Pagano to step away from the team to undergo treatment. The team continued on and played for its ailing coach. Led by interim head coach Bruce Arians,

One young Colts fan shows her support for head coach Chuck Pagano as he underwent treatment for leukemia.

the Colts battled to an 11–5 record. That was good enough to get back to the playoffs. Even better, after chemotherapy treatments Pagano's cancer was in remission. Pagano returned for the regular-season finale, a victory over Houston that secured the top wild-card spot in the AFC playoffs. The next week, the Colts lost 24–9 to the Baltimore Ravens, who went on to win that year's Super Bowl.

Luck continued to improve in his second season. After throwing 18 interceptions as a rookie, he only threw nine in 2013. In Week 7 of that season, Luck and the Colts took on their old friend Manning, who was now quarterbacking the Denver Broncos. Luck defeated his predecessor 39–33. Indianapolis went on to finish the season 11–5 and win the AFC South title.

In the wild-card round, Indianapolis hosted the Kansas City Chiefs. Little went right for the Colts early on. After Luck threw an interception to start the second half, the Chiefs took a 38–10 lead. But the Colts would not go quietly. Luck threw three touchdown passes in the second half to help lead an incredible comeback. He even recovered a teammate's fumble and scrambled into the end zone for a score.

Luck's final touchdown pass of the day was a 64-yard strike to T. Y. Hilton that put Indianapolis ahead 45–44 with 4:29 to play. The defense stopped the Chiefs, and the Colts clinched a wild victory. At the time, it was the second-largest comeback in NFL playoff history.

The next season, the Colts went one step further, beating Manning and the Broncos in the divisional playoffs to reach the

Luck throws deep against the Chiefs in the Colts' epic playoff comeback in January 2014. Luck threw for 443 yards and four touchdowns in the 45–44 win.

AFC Championship Game. The Colts faced a tough challenge at New England. For the second straight season, the Patriots ended the Colts' season, this time with a 45–7 rout.

Still, things were looking up for the Colts. Luck was only 25 years old after the 2014 season, and he had already led the team to the playoffs three times. Indianapolis appeared poised to be a Super Bowl contender for many years to come. But that proved not to be the case.

Colts wide receiver T. Y. Hilton catches a touchdown pass against the Buffalo Bills in 2018.

Luck began having problems with his throwing shoulder starting in 2015. Luck missed 10 games during the next two seasons as the injury lingered. The Colts went 8–8 both years. In 2017 the injury forced Luck to miss the entire season. Indianapolis finished 4–12 and fired Pagano. After missing 26 of 48 games over three seasons, Luck was confident he would return fully healthy in 2018.

The Colts went into the offseason looking for an offense-minded head coach who could work with Luck. They hired Frank Reich, a longtime NFL backup quarterback who spent eight years behind Hall of Famer Jim Kelly in Buffalo. Reich came to Indianapolis after winning a Super Bowl as the Philadelphia Eagles' offensive coordinator.

Reich and Luck proved to be a good match. Finally healthy, Luck returned in 2018 with one of his best seasons. His 4,593 passing yards and 39 touchdown passes were both just shy of his career bests. Meanwhile, in 2018 Reich helped the Indianapolis offense rebound from thirtieth in the NFL to fifth in points scored.

Having won eight of their previous nine games, the Colts went into Week 17 with a 9–6 record. They needed to beat the Tennessee Titans in order to secure the AFC's last wild-card spot. And that's what they did, winning 33–17.

The red-hot Colts went on the road to start the playoffs and dominated the Houston Texans 21–7. But that's as far as the playoff run extended. The next week, in Kansas City against another red-hot team, the Colts lost 31–13. But with an innovative new coach and a star quarterback in his prime, the future appeared bright in Indianapolis.

TIMELINE

1953
On January 23, the Baltimore Colts enter the league, replacing the Dallas Texans, who folded the previous season.

1958
On December 28, Baltimore defeats the New York Giants 23–17 in overtime to win the NFL Championship in one of the most important games in pro football history.

1959
Baltimore repeats as NFL champions, defeating the Giants 31–16 at Memorial Stadium on December 27.

1964
Cleveland defeats Baltimore 27–0 in the NFL Championship Game on December 27.

1968
Baltimore defeats Cleveland 34–0 to win the NFL Championship on December 29.

1969
A crowd of 75,389 watches one of the greatest upsets in pro football history as the New York Jets defeat the Colts 16–7 in Super Bowl III on January 12.

1971
Jim O'Brien kicks a 32-yard field goal in the last seconds of Super Bowl V to lift Baltimore past the Dallas Cowboys 16–13 on January 17.

1984
On March 28, Colts owner Robert Irsay moves the team from Baltimore to Indianapolis in the middle of the night.

1987
The Colts make the playoffs for the first time in 10 years by winning the AFC East.

1995
The Colts defeat the San Diego Chargers 35–20 on December 31 to earn the franchise's first playoff victory since moving from Baltimore.

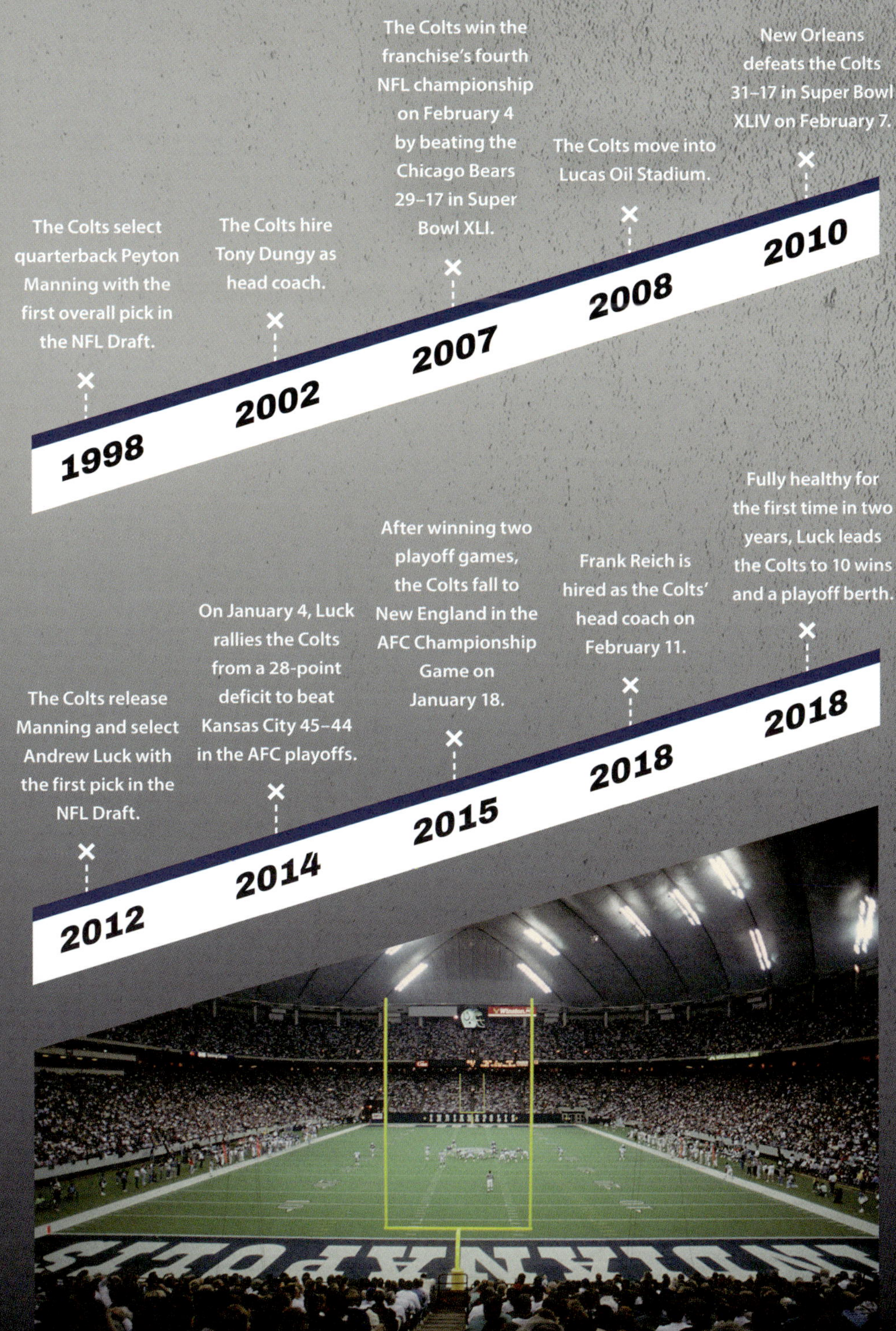

1998
The Colts select quarterback Peyton Manning with the first overall pick in the NFL Draft.

2002
The Colts hire Tony Dungy as head coach.

2007
The Colts win the franchise's fourth NFL championship on February 4 by beating the Chicago Bears 29–17 in Super Bowl XLI.

2008
The Colts move into Lucas Oil Stadium.

2010
New Orleans defeats the Colts 31–17 in Super Bowl XLIV on February 7.

2012
The Colts release Manning and select Andrew Luck with the first pick in the NFL Draft.

2014
On January 4, Luck rallies the Colts from a 28-point deficit to beat Kansas City 45–44 in the AFC playoffs.

2015
After winning two playoff games, the Colts fall to New England in the AFC Championship Game on January 18.

2018
Frank Reich is hired as the Colts' head coach on February 11.

2018
Fully healthy for the first time in two years, Luck leads the Colts to 10 wins and a playoff berth.

QUICK STATS

FRANCHISE HISTORY

Baltimore Colts (1953–83)
Indianapolis Colts (1984–)

SUPER BOWLS *(wins in bold)*

1968 (III), **1970 (V)**, **2006 (XLI)**, 2009 (XLIV)

NFL CHAMPIONSHIP GAMES *(1953–69; wins in bold)*

1958, **1959**, 1964, **1968**

AFC CHAMPIONSHIP GAMES *(since 1970 AFL-NFL merger)*

1970, 1971, 1995, 2003, 2006, 2009, 2014

KEY COACHES

Tony Dungy (2002–08): 85–27, 7–6 (playoffs)
Weeb Ewbank (1954–62): 59–52–1, 2–0 (playoffs)
Don Shula (1963–69): 71–23–4, 2–3 (playoffs)

KEY PLAYERS *(position, seasons with team)*

Raymond Berry (WR, 1955–67)
Dallas Clark (TE, 2003–11)
Eric Dickerson (RB, 1987–91)
Art Donovan (DT, 1950, 1953–61)
Dwight Freeney (DE, 2002–12)
Marvin Harrison (WR, 1996–2008)
T. Y. Hilton (WR, 2012–)
Edgerrin James (RB, 1999–2005)
Bert Jones (QB, 1973–81)
Andrew Luck (QB, 2012–)
John Mackey (TE, 1963–71)
Peyton Manning (QB, 1998–2011)
Gino Marchetti (DE, 1953–64, 1966)
Lenny Moore (RB, 1956–67)
Jim Parker (OL, 1957–67)
Jeff Saturday (C, 1999–2011)
Johnny Unitas (QB, 1956–72)
Reggie Wayne (WR, 2001–14)

HOME FIELDS

(in Indianapolis)
Lucas Oil Stadium (2008–)
RCA Dome (1984–2007)
Also known as Hoosier Dome
(in Baltimore)
Memorial Stadium (1953–83)

*All statistics through 2018 season

QUOTES AND ANECDOTES

From 1998 to 2010, Peyton Manning started every game for the Colts. Other NFL teams have not been as fortunate. During that span, the other 31 NFL teams combined to use 339 different starting quarterbacks. The Chicago Bears started 17 different players at quarterback between 1998 and 2010, while the Cleveland Browns and Miami Dolphins each used 16 different starting quarterbacks during that time.

"There's a big difference between confidence and conceit. To me, conceit is bragging about yourself. Being confident means you believe you can get the job done, but you know you can't get your job done unless you also have the confidence that the other guys are going to get their jobs done too. Without them, I'm nothing."

—Johnny Unitas on accusations that his confidence was a reflection of his arrogance

When Don Shula was named coach of the Baltimore Colts, he was the youngest head coach in the NFL. During his Pro Football Hall of Fame induction speech, Shula recalled a meeting with Carroll Rosenbloom, the owner of the Colts at the time. "He said, 'You're going to be the youngest coach in the National Football League. Do you think that you're ready for the job?' And I said, 'Carroll, the only way that you'll find out is if you hire me and give me the opportunity.' He liked that answer; he gave me the job."

In 2013 Indianapolis selected defensive end Bjoern Werner with its first-round draft pick. It wasn't a flashy pick at the time. But Werner came in with an interesting story. He grew up in Germany and started playing football as a foreign exchange student in Connecticut as a high schooler. Werner played three years with the Colts and retired from football in 2017.

GLOSSARY

clinch
Finalize a series victory, division title, or wild card spot.

comeback
A rally by a team losing a game tie the score or take the lead.

disband
To break something up, such as a sports franchise.

dominant
Consistently better than an opponent.

draft
A system that allows teams to acquire new players coming into a league.

franchise
A sports organization, including the top-level team and all minor league affiliates.

media
Various forms of communication, including television, radio, and newspapers; the press or news reporting agencies.

replacement players
Players brought in while others are on strike.

retire
To end one's career.

rival
An opponent with whom a player or team has a fierce and ongoing competition.

rookie
A professional athlete in his or her first year of competition.

strike
A work stoppage by employees in protest of working conditions.

MORE INFORMATION

BOOKS

Kortemeier, Todd. *Indianapolis Colts*. Minneapolis, MN: Abdo Publishing, 2017.

Scheff, Matt. *Andrew Luck*. Minneapolis, MN: Abdo Publishing, 2016.

Scheff, Matt. *Peyton Manning*. Minneapolis, MN: Abdo Publishing, 2016.

ONLINE RESOURCES

To learn more about the Indianapolis Colts, visit **abdobooklinks.com** or scan this QR code. These links are routinely monitored and updated to provide the most current information available.

PLACE TO VISIT

Grand Park Sports Campus
19000 Grand Park Blvd.
Westfield, IN 46074
317-804-3010
grandpark.org

The site of the annual Colts training camp hosts more than just football. The 400-acre sports complex has 26 baseball and softball fields and 31 fields for either soccer, football, or lacrosse.

INDEX

Addai, Joseph, 8, 31
Ameche, Alan, 13
Arians, Bruce, 36

Berry, Raymond, 20

Caldwell, Jim, 33
Clark, Dallas, 30
Curtis, Mike, 20

Dickerson, Eric, 24–25, 26
Donovan, Art, 20
Dungy, Tony, 9, 32–33

Ewbank, Weeb, 12, 15, 18

Faulk, Marshall, 26
Freeney, Dwight, 33

Grigson, Ryan, 36

Harbaugh, Jim, 25
Harrison, Marvin, 30
Hayden, Kelvin, 8
Hilton, T. Y., 38

Irsay, Robert, 22

James, Edgerrin, 30–31
Jones, Bert, 21

Luck, Andrew, 36, 38–41

Mackey, John, 19, 20
Manning, Peyton, 4–6, 8, 28–31, 32, 33, 34–36, 38
Marchetti, Gino, 20
Marchibroda, Ted, 21, 25
McCafferty, Don, 18
Moore, Lenny, 20
Mora, Jim, 28, 31–32
Morrall, Earl, 16
Myhra, Steve, 13

Nowatzke, Tom, 20

O'Brien, Jim, 20

Pagano, Chuck, 36–37, 40
Parker, Jim, 20

Reich, Frank, 41
Rhodes, Dominic, 8

Sanders, Bob, 33
Shula, Don, 15, 16–18

Unitas, Johnny, 13, 15, 16–21

Vinatieri, Adam, 6, 7–8

Wayne, Reggie, 7, 30, 36

ABOUT THE AUTHOR

Robert Cooper is a retired law enforcement officer and lifelong NFL fan. He and his wife live in Seattle near their only son and two grandchildren